Grieving Forward

Grieving Forward

Embracing Each Moment with God
Devotions for Living Life after Loss

SHAWANDA THAMES PAYNE

Unless otherwise specified, all scripture quotations are taken from the King James Version of the Bible and New Living Translation

ISBN 978-1-7328178-0-7

Photograph by J Raphael Photography

Cover design: Brand It Beautifully with Allison Denise

Printed in the United States of America

Published by Shawanda Thames Payne

spayne-2@hotmail.com

Contents

Foreword

In this literary work, you can expect to be truly encouraged and enlightened by the thoughts of Shawanda Payne. She will help you to understand that in the human experience of life grief certainly plays a part. She explains that loss is a part of life and grief is a natural response to loss.

How wonderfully she conveys that overcoming grief is addressed by expressing it to God. She as well helps us to know that having the right perspective is an overcoming tool in addressing the matter of grief.

Allow the words of her mouth and the meditation of her heart to be acceptable in your hearing as well as your heart. You will be reminded that weeping endures for a night and joy comes in the morning. Tell your grief, its morning time as you read this book!!!

Bishop Roderick Mitchell

Dedication

I dedicate this book to my parents, Diane and John Thames. Thank you both for naturally birthing my sister and raising her to be a God-fearing woman and an amazing big sister. Thank you for moving forward in life after the loss of your oldest child and allowing the Lord to lead you both to healing and restoration. Thank you for demonstrating that even in suffering you can still serve and trust God. I pray that the oil of joy and the garment of praise rest on you daily. I love you both!

I dedicate this book to my siblings, Shakesha and Lil John. I appreciate you both for making our sibling unity solid. Our childhood, adult experiences, and upbringing made us appreciate and love each other more. I love you both dearly.

This book is dedicated to my niece, Sa'Nya, thank you for sharing your Mommy with us. You have many beautiful characteristics of her, and I love watching you grow. Your sweet presence and life is a gift to our family. I love you greatly!

Acknowledgements

I give all the glory to God for the opportunity to hear His voice to encourage to His people through my personal experience of life after the loss. I am grateful that I gained many moments to embrace, Abba, My Father!

Thanks to Marcus Payne, my husband, for believing in me and never complaining about the many sacrifices we made while working and investing on this God-given vision. Thanks for being a listening ear and pushing me on this entire journey. Thank you, Jeremiah, Marcus, and Sean, my sons, for being a huge part of my motivation, especially when the grief moments seemed unbearable in the beginning. Thank you for your smiles, laughter, and keeping me busy with raising you. You boys are an amazing blessing to my life.

Thank you, Dr. Brenda Randle, The Writing Doctor, for coaching me in working the vision and birthing the vision. Thank you for your proficiency in editing. Thank You for every piece of assistance given on this journey. I was drowning in grief, and God used you to push me into purpose. I am forever grateful for your prayers, encouragement, and pushing me in one of the most uncomfortable seasons in my life.

Many thanks to my spiritual leaders, Pastor Jonathan Brown and Co-Pastor Ashely Brown of The Carpenters Church for providing me the spiritual nourishment I need for my deliverance, healing, and growth. I am grateful for your spiritual support through counseling, teaching, preaching, encouragement, prayers, and love.

Thank you Bishop Roderick Mitchell and Pastor Mary Mitchell for taking spiritual care of my sister while she lived on this earth. I appreciate you both for praying for my family and for making this process as smooth as possible. I learned much from you both.

Thank you a million to my family Derrick and Mary Rogers. Thank you for believing in me. Thank you for the support of your generous donations, input, and listening ear. Special thanks to my family, special friends, my prayer partners for the support and cheering me on.

Thanks to J Raphael Photography for your amazing work in photography. The entire process was fun, smooth, and rememberable.

Thank you, Brand it Beautifully with Allison Denise for your excellence in book cover designing and interior formatting.

Thank you, Sharetta Small Donaldson, Author of *Forgiveness: A Quest for Healing Your Heart*. Thank you for your selflessness on this journey.

Also, thank you Shemeka Washington, Author of *The Exchange: Beauty for Ashes* for your encouragement and assistance.

Huge thanks to my readers! I appreciate you for your support and for investing your time into reading my personal experience and allowing it me to encourage you as God intended.

Preface

Grief is not a good feeling, which is followed by great turbulence; however, I have found that valuable lessons can be found in the most hurtful pain, even the deepest parts of grief. Finding the good in the hardest circumstances of grief can help you move forward after loss. Oftentimes, we are weighed down to search for the good in our adversity. Walk with me through my journey of grief as I give the transparent highs and lows of my grieving forward experiences.

I would like to share this book with anyone who is struggling to go on with their life after the death of a loved one. You may be at the point of giving up or not sure where to start. Do not feel alone because there are many of us who have and who are having a difficult time moving forward after the loss of a loved one. Allow me to shed light on many practical examples of finding meaning in loss.

Many people grieve and have no idea of how to grieve in a healthy way. You may be wondering how to balance your grief and daily life responsibilities. You may be seeking a deeper relationship with God after you have experienced the loss of a loved one and unsure of how to feed your grieving spirit. There may be a loved one or friend that you wish to help on their grief journey. I pray that this devotional will be used as a practical resource to uplift someone during their time of grief.

My own grief journey has caused me to become aware and more sensitive to the many people holding the unspoken pain of grief in their hearts. Even though we all grieve in our own way, we somehow share commonalities in our grief process. God has given me an increased ability to empathize with others, even in my own hurt. Knowing firsthand what it is like to hurt after the loss of a loved one can be helpful to another person who is grieving.

Allow me to be a voice for you as you read each word and to provide you with spiritual comfort through my transparent experiences, encouragement, and prayers. Open your heart and mind and share this journey with me. Like many, God made it possible for me to strive daily to live my life after an unexpected and significant loss. My hope is to inspire and to motivate you to embrace each grieving forward moment. May you be strengthened to move forward and regain peace, joy, comfort, support, balance, and healing.

I want to enlighten you of how God is guarding my heart and my mind as much as I need Him to in every step of my grief journey. In the early stages on my grief journey, I recited to the Lord many times a day, *"Your grace is sufficient for me" (2 Corinthians 12:9)*. God's grace is sufficient, and His power is made perfect in your weakness, in your brokenness, and in your weariness. My prayer is that you allow His Strength to be made perfect in your weakness. I knew that grief after my sister's death was something I couldn't avoid. So, I longed for more of Him and His fulfillment and less of my hurt and pain due to the grief I was going through.

I had many concerns and fears as I dealt with my own personal grief. The many unwanted feelings of grief weighed me down. During those moments, I remembered that God says that we should give our cares and worries to Him because He cares for us *(1 Peter 5:7)*. The Bible tells us, *"The Lord will perfect everything that which concerns us and His mercy endures forever (Psalm 138:8)*. I was sure that He was not looking out for just me, but also those that were being affected by my sister's death and the many that has experienced the passing of a loved one. I gave it all to our Heavenly Father because the pain was too much for me to bear alone. I could not move physically, mentally, or spiritually without my Heavenly Father.

I have grown in my spiritual walk with Christ. I pray that as you read this devotional book that you will develop a deeper trust in God and a greater reliance on Him as your source of comfort. I decided to move forward in my life, even though I experienced a great loss with the uncertainty of what was to come after. I wanted to serve the Lord regardless. My grief journey is a testament and confirmation that I am sold out for Christ. My desire is for complete wholeness and healing for myself and those who have experience the loss a loved one. I know the kind of God I serve, and how He has always been my Provider. He is a faithful and a loving God. God sent His loving son Jesus, so that we can all have the opportunity to be saved, set free, and delivered. Jesus purpose is to give us *a rich and satisfying life (John 10:10).* I searched for life after a great loss, and I have found a greater sense of purpose. As a follower of Christ, I can share this with others who grieve due to loss. It was during the process of my grief journey that I was able to experience God's powerful hands of protection, peace, and comfort.

Although no words, written or spoken, can take the pain away, allow this devotional to feed your soul with comfort, encouragement, and prayer. I pray that you would benefit from reading my personal experiences and that you would receive my heartfelt encouragements throughout each page of how my loss changed into a renewed spiritual gain in Christ. I challenge you to utilize the scriptures and prayers as a means of a deeper communion with God. Meditate and recite them to build your faith and a deeper confidence in God.

Shawanda Payne

Introduction

After going through many challenges in life, I often wondered what could be worse. When I least expected it, I received an unwanted call about my sister's death. Years ago, I made the decision to give my life to Christ. Unknowingly, the death of my sister and grieving became the highpoint for my spiritual walk with God. My sister's sickness started my grief journey and my new life of renewed strength, hope, and courage to moving forward after loss.

I have had my share of trials and tribulations. However, nothing can compare to how I felt immediately after receiving the news of my sister's death. My life changed significantly. We all will experience loss and pain in life. It all depends on how we focus our attention on God, who has the power to overturn our adversities of grief to healing. It was in each moment of the difficulties and struggles of grief that I was able to experience God's power. It has been well over three years ago since my dear sister's death, and I am now on a journey that I was not prepared to take. However, God has chosen this path for me. This was not my initial response, but her death and grief has opened my eyes and understanding to a deeper dependency on Christ. I encourage you to *"trust in the Lord with all your heart; do not depend on your own understanding" (Proverbs 3:5, NLT).*

It is my God-given purpose to share my testimony through this devotional and to offer encouragement and comfort to the pain you are feeling. I have been inspired by God's power and His wonderful works to share my sister's life, her transition from earth to heaven, and my personal grief experiences to write this book. God has ordered my steps in this process. My grief journey has been challenging, yet I have a discovered a deeper appreciation for God's miraculous works and His fulfilling presence. I needed His comforting presence during the hardest times of my grief and continue to depend on Him greatly.

My experience of loss shares how all areas of my life were tested by my grief challenges. The spiritual aspect of my life was tested, yet aided me through my grief process and helped me to overcome my grief fears. I looked forward to gaining spiritual knowledge and wisdom to move forward in my daily life as I deal with my living my life without my dear sister. Proverbs 3:6 says to *"Seek His will in all you do and He will show you which path to take."*(NLT). My significant loss led me to seek God's will more than ever before. I felt completely devastated after the loss of my sister, yet my soul desired life after loss. The death of my sister left me heartbroken and lost. Grief pushed me into a place where I needed to be rescued by God Almighty, my refuge and my fortress.

I had never experienced the magnitude of peace as I did after my sister's passing. The moment I found out that she was gone, I experienced another level of God's peace that consumed me. It was only by God's grace and His strength that our family was strengthen and could actively engage in celebrating her life while going through the process and preparations of laying our loved one to rest.

Grievers maybe unaware that there is a process to their healing. Many think that it is not acceptable to move forward and live an abundant life after loss. I pray that as I share my grief experience after the loss of sister that it paves the way for others to move forward with Christ to accept the process of their grief that brings true healing and wholeness. I am hoping that my readers find the peace, strength, and the comfort they need in Christ.

I found rest in the safety of God's Word. The wisdom in the Scriptures gave me hope and the necessary strength to go forth. Reading and meditating on Scriptures was a coping skill that provided me the encouragement I needed throughout the day, while also praying as often as I could. I discovered a new wisdom in the Scriptures. Even in my grief, I hungered and thirst for God. This way of coping gave me life and a reason to live again, even after losing my first sister, my first friend, and my confidant.

My hope is to increase the awareness of grief, and discuss how grief affects a grievers' physical, mental, social, emotional, and spiritual well-being by utilizing my own personal experience and testimony.

Grieving is necessary to the individual's pathway to healing. Grieving moments are the defining times of where your efforts to heal are vital. I want to open the door for others to share their genuine feelings about grief. My prayer is to break the barriers and light the torch for other grievers who are afraid and uncomfortable with openly sharing their grief. My prayer is that you are filled with inspiration as you grieve forward to healing. May God's peace bring light, even in the darkest moments of your grieving time.

1

Knowledge of Grief

"Hold on to instruction, do not let it go: guard it well, for it is your life." -Proverbs 4:13 (NIV)

~PRAYER to PRAY~

Heavenly Father, I come to You right now to thank You for this new journey of grief. Please take my hand as I go through this process of grief. I admit that I do not know how to deal with grief, but I trust You to lead and guide me every step of the way. I know that You are with me. Direct me to the proper knowledge, people, and resources. Lead me to the caring people that will provide the necessary support. I desire to become more knowledgeable about grief, grieving, and loss. I trust You to carry me through, even in the darkest moments. In Jesus Name, Amen.

I graduated from Delta State University with a Bachelor of Social Work degree. As a college student, I gained knowledge about death, dying, and grief stages. It is eleven years later, and still those courses have been a valuable influence in my life. Unknowingly, I was being prepared to deal with my own personal experience of death and grief. Fortunately, the knowledge I obtained through my education resulted in me being knowledgeable in knowing what to expect while grieving. The educational tools to coping with grief during my college years were beneficial to coping with losing my dear sister. The knowledge I received has been enlightening on this journey.

The choice to read many books that educates you to deal with grief is highly effective when trying to understand grief. In a greatly influential book, *On Grief and Grieving: Finding the Meaning of Grief through the Five Stages of Loss (2005)*, Elisabeth Kubler-Ross and David Kessler discuss the process of grieving and use theory, inspiration, and practical advice while utilizing their own professional and personal experiences. The authors discuss "the five stages of grief, which are part of the background that make up our learning to live with the one we lost. These stages are denial, anger, bargaining, depression, and acceptance. The grief process can be used as tools to help us frame and identify what we may be feeling."

Please understand that there is no set time of how to grieve. Elisabeth Kubler-Ross and David Kessler stated that "not everyone goes through all of the stages of grief or goes in a prescribed order." Awareness of the grief stages helped me to understand what I was going through after the loss of my sister. I was well informed of what I was going through. I did not enjoy the feelings of grieving, but I understood the significance of grief.

While grieving, it is normal to feel like you do not understand what is going on while you are going through the grieving process. Everyone's grief process is different. The more significant the loss, the more intense the grief process can be. Intense grief can cause a person to experience physical symptoms such as fatigue, shortness of breath, dizziness, palpitations, and feelings of numbness, irritability, restlessness, headaches, stomachache, appetite loss, and the inability to organize daily activities. The feelings of intense grief were what seemed to be too much to bear. Many days, I thought I was going "crazy". That was a part of the grief process. Allowing myself to go through the stages has caused me to learn that a Greater Source of strength was working in me. So, remember that when you are weak, God is strong enough to carry you through the toughest moments.

Grief is not an enjoyable journey, but eventually new life is re-invented. Many others have gone through the journey of grief and many others will. Your stages of grief will not be the same as the next person or mine. It is an individual process; however, we all find some connections in grief.

Through each moment of my grief, I was confident that God was with me. Joshua 1:9 says to be "strong *and courageous. Do not be afraid or discouraged. For the Lord your God is with you wherever you go" (NLT).*

This was my hope and strength. I held God's word in my heart. I understand and I accept that my life will not be as it was before my sister passed. Her dying unexpectedly changed my life and grief allowed me to find new life after loss.

The Word of God allows me to know the significance of Jesus Christ and His power to work in us.

You can have joy. Learning new ways of living without the physical presence of your loved one is a challenge. There is hope in Christ and living life, so accept the strength that you need on your journey.

On Grief and Grieving: Finding the Meaning of Grief through the Five Stages of Loss (2005), Elisabeth Kubler-Ross and David Kessler describe grief stages as "responses to feelings that can last for minutes or hours as we flip in and out of one and then another. We do not enter and leave each individual stage in a linear fashion. We may feel one, then another, and back again."

Grief takes work from the griever to begin healing. You have to be willing to become knowledgeable about grief and your own individual grief process. You have to accept that this is a journey you don't have to go through alone. I encourage you to work through your grief. Take your pain and suffering caused by loss and give it to your Heavenly Father.

I took my hurt and pain after losing my sister and decided to work towards taking charge of my healing by relying on God's Word and His promises to direct my path in each step. God can and will heal you after loss through the power of prayer and by allowing Him on your grief journey. He is available to make you whole. The Holy Spirit will teach you how to live after the loss of your loved one.

2

God's Timing

"There is a time for everything, and a season for every activity under the heavens: A time to be born and a time to die, a time to plant and a time to uproot."

Ecclesiastes 3:1-2 (NIV)

~PRAYER to PRAY~

Lord, I may not understand Your timing, but I trust that You are with me on this journey of grief. I want to embrace Your timing, and I desire to feel your comfort during this difficult and unexpected time. I know that You are with me in every step on this journey. I give You my fears and my uncertainties trusting that You will heal my grieving heart. I believe in Your power to heal hurting hearts. Your goodness and faithfulness keeps me grounded. Your grace and mercy is everlasting. Thank You Father. In Jesus name, Amen.

"If something was to happen to Ninni (my sister), I don't know what I would do." A statement I made many times in my life as I often spoke about my sister while referring to the closeness of our relationship. Her illness marked the onset of my grief journey. Even as she grew weary in her body, I did not want to accept the fact that death could possibly occur.

The challenges that a family face when confronted with a loved one's illness are always difficult. The family's structure and dynamics change, while learning to cope with setbacks and other changes as family member battles with a life-changing illness. We worked together as a family to assure that my sister had a support system. We were afraid of what could happened.

I lived my life knowing that I would wake up and be able to call my sister. I always figured that she would be available to me all the time. Basically, we had each other's back. We had many conversations on how we would raise our children together. That I would be her matron of honor in her wedding. That we will always have time together. My hope was that she would go into the hospital and come out in better health as happened many times before. Two weeks prior to her dying, avoiding the fact that she could possibly die, I went about the days of her hospitalization feeling scared, but hopeful she would make it.

My heart grieved each time her illness had an effect on her daily living and caused her to be hospitalized. Life seemed unfair. Sometimes, I could barely go to work, let alone focus on work, daily interactions, and routines in my life. However, I continued with my life by keeping busy, loving on her, being the best sister I thought I could be, while avoiding the reality of death.

In 2010, she was diagnosed with postpartum cardio myopathy, an uncommon form of heart failure that happens during the last month of pregnancy or up to five months after giving birth. She was diagnosed six months after giving birth to her daughter and battled for six years before dying at the age of 33. I watched her fight in the most difficult times while she dealt with this heart condition. At the time, I did not understood how she was able to handle this course in the graceful manner she did.

I felt horrible and helpless. She was a good person, sweet, and selfless. Many times, I wished I were the one dealing with the pain instead. This was also a part of my grieving process, which is a normal stage of grief called bargaining. I was also angry. At the time, I thought that life was cruel and unfair.

I got a phone call from the surgeon saying, "Shanika had complications after heart surgery and the family needed to get there soon." At this point, I was faced with what I had avoided for six years; that my big sister, one of the closest person to me, could leave this earth. Forever! I balled myself in my work chair and cried loud and hard. I lost control of the emotions I held in for six years. Once I finally got myself together, I left work feeling that life will change forever.

Not even an hour later, I received a second call. It was the surgeon again. Somehow, I felt that it was not going to be something good. I remember the surgeon saying with extreme disappointment and sadness in his voice, "I'm sorry, we tried all that we could", which sent me into a state of shock. I did not hear anything else. What I experienced next were the feelings of shock, which gave me enough cushion to get through the initial mourning process. I had to get to my mother, my other sister, niece, and other family members to check on them. It was all happening so fast. My daddy and brother were out of town. I felt responsible to make sure my family was together to deal with my sister's unexpected death. I hid my feelings to avoid the intense feelings of grief. I was numb. The numbness helped me to ride two hours away to go see my sister's lifeless body and to begin the preparation to plan her funeral.

I thought that my sister's death came much too soon. I was faced with my own unwanted personal experience with loss while being afraid and unsure of what would happen next. I hid the feelings of pain that I would soon have to endure. Even though the pain was great, I realize that I did not have any control over God's timing for my sister's transition from earth to heaven. I realized that my desires for her life to suite my desires were not in God's plan for her life. The more I reflect on my sister's passing, I recall her, in her own way, trying to tell me that she would not be with us long. At the time, I missed it. I was not ready. The thought of her dying created anxiety and fear within me. Knowing that her illness was severe enough to cause death caused me great pain.

Grief is a natural reaction and a response to loss or a change of any kind. It affects every dimension of our being: physical, mental, emotional, and spiritual. Loss is a fact of life, and so are the reactions that follow. Allow the natural reactions and responses of grief to take its course in your life. During these times, the Lord will strengthen you and provide you with all the necessary comfort you need to pull through each moment.

God's timing is His timing. Know that God's timing is perfect. Trust in His goodness. God's patience and timing must not be mistaken for His absence. His presence is constant. Yes, even after loss. Knowing that He is always with us gave me much assurance and comfort as my grief journey unfolded. God can heal a grieving spirit. Allow God to heal your spirit through the power of prayer and faith.

3

Resting in His Presence

"Come to me, all who are weary and burdened, and I will give you rest." *-Matthew 11:28 (NIV)*

~PRAYER to PRAY~

Father, I thank You for allowing me to rest in Your presence, even during the most difficult time in my life. I accept You as my personal Savior. It brings me great joy that I can give You my concerns of grief. I realize that without You I would not receive the rest and peace I need to move forward. I rest in Your presence. I welcome Your love and peace to comfort me. I rest in the assurance of knowing that You are God and God alone. Thank You Heavenly Father. In Jesus' name, Amen.

The painful realization of losing a loved one can feel like you have been hit with a full force of great emotion and physical pain. Emotional feelings, such as loss of appetite, sadness, and anxiety, began to consume me deeply. At that point, I found myself heavily burdened and weary in my body, mind, and spirit. I felt like I was going to lose my mind and total control of life.

I realized that the death of my sister and my grief experience was beyond my control. I did not want to believe that she was gone. I knew it, I heard the surgeon say it. I just could not believe it. It was too much for me to bear.

The stage of denial helped me get through in the beginning, wondering if maybe the call was only a dream. I felt like I was floating. In all honesty, denial was a way for me to get through the hardest steps of preparing my sister's funeral. It was all true. It was not a dream. She was gone.

I realized that the help that I needed was more powerful than death, grief, and self. I wondered how could I go on with my life and why should I go on. The very thing that I did not want to happen has happened. WHAT NOW? This process of grief I was experiencing was denial. I would say to family and close friends, "I keep thinking she is not gone." I was burdened over the reality that she was not coming back, which was a hard reality to think or live through.

It was difficult to confront the realness of seeing her lifeless body and making decisions as we prepared to lay her body to rest. The grace of God allowed me to manage the feelings of denial for a little while. It was not long before I had to make a decision.

My decision was to depend on God as I accept the reality of loss. I wanted to rest more than anything. If I did not rest, I knew my mind would not be in any condition to make sound decisions. We had a funeral to arrange. So one moment I prayed for rest, another I prayed for peace and strength. The wonderful working power of God's grace provided me with the rest and peace that I needed to move forward. I became stronger and the denial began to diminish.

Our bodies are sensitive and responding to loss can affect your body, mind, and spirit. Listen to your body. It is normal to have trouble sleeping during times of grief. God wants you to take care of yourself. It is of great importance that you rest more during your grief process.

In dealing with grief, there is no set timeline to going through the stages of grief. I was determined not to allow the hurt and pain of my sister's death to diminish my ability to feel God's presence. I was determined to rest at night and have peace; even in my deepest hurt.

I encourage you today to rest in God's Presence. I assure you that He will take care of you as you rest and rise for whatever you have to handle in this day. He knows that grief is too much of a burden for you to carry. He's there to bring you out of every agony caused by loss and grief moments. Cry out to Him in prayer, and He will give your heart and soul desire of rest. *"Take delight in the Lord and He will give you your heart's desires" (Psalms 37:4, NLT).*

If you have not accepted Jesus Christ as your Savior, I encourage you to search your heart and make that choice. You do not have to go through grief alone. God is the necessary route for your healing due to loss. You can survive loss, grief, and the heartaches it brings. God will grant you peace in the process and even as you get to your place of acceptance and healing.

4

Comfort in the Mourning

"Blessed are those who mourn, for they will be comforted." -Matthew 5:4 (NIV)

~PRAYER to PRAY~

Father, I thank You for Your continuous support. Thank You for sending others to console and comfort me during the hard times of my grieving process. Your blessings are present even in these times. I thank You for the comfort that You provide me as I arise each day. Enhance my walk with You as I go this difficult process. I need You and cannot get along without You. Your comfort keeps me and gives me the peace I need. Thank You, Father. In Jesus' name, Amen.

The comfort of our Heavenly Father is greater than we can ever imagine. His love lasts forever. At the beginning of my grief journey, there were many family, close friends, and others that offered support in their unique ways. I truly believe that Jesus sends others to show love and compassion as He would. They are truly sent by God with a purpose to comfort with much empathy, compassion, and encouragement.

No words could console the heartbreak I felt after the death of my big sister. Honestly, words were not enough to help how I felt. Some words just were not comforting or genuine. However, the many expressions of care, compassion, and support were appreciated and heartfelt. Many of the visits were awkward during the beginning. The feeling of being alone to deal with grief was frightening. At some points, I was able to manage daily responsibilities because I wanted to stay busy. There were many times, I needed to sit, lay in bed to cry, or rest. The support of others is vital to your healing process.

Mourning requires the support of others for you to heal. God provides comfort and gives us the support conducive to our grief needs. Dealing with grief on your own can be lonely and unhealthy. We need others on this journey. The comfort and support they provide is vital on this journey. Most times, you may find yourself dependent on others to get you through the pain.

Take time to yourself, but time with others is needed more than ever. It is okay to find support in other family members, close friends, your church family, and new people. Grief has a way of strengthening families and friendships and even forming new friendships. The emotional support from family and friends being available when we needed them was a blessing.

Unfortunately, family and friends will have to go back home to their own lives. You will be left to face your own feelings of grief. I was scared, lost, and felt helpless. I felt alone. A deep sadness settled in my soul. I cried alone. I wanted out of the feelings of despair and sadness, and I did not know how long I would feel this way.

The need of a spiritual support system is vital. You will need to attend church service to be in the midst of other believers. Allow your spiritual leaders to pray with you. Don't be afraid to reach out and request and receive prayer from trusted people.

I realize now that my people of support were not aware of how deeply my grief affected me. At this point, the ability to accept the vital need of the comforting support from *"The Comforter" (John 14:26, KJV)* and other people is greatly accepted and appreciated. I encourage you to reach out and accept your support system. Allow the support of others to be an on-going part of your grief journey.

The process of grief is complicated and involves many feelings: sadness, confusion, a desire to be alone, anxiety, and helplessness. It benefits to have others around to console and provide support. Allow your friends and family to express their support in their unique ways. However, do not hesitate to be honest about your needs. Ask for help. Let people help and be open to receiving during this period. Share your feelings and thoughts of grief. Take breaks to yourself and allow your support system to provide you with some relief.

God provides us with what and who we need to get through the toughest stages in your grief. He sends others to offer us emotional, physical, and spiritual support. The comfort of others is an essential part of the healing process.

Grief is a long-term process, and some days will be good and some bad. The dark days were rougher than I could ever imagine. This was all necessary and a normal part of grieving. Do not avoid it, ignore it, or suppress it. As long as your emotions are moving and changing, your grief is on track. Allow the grief to take you where you need to go. Search for God in your hardest times of grief and you will find Him to be a *"Resting Place" (Isaiah 28:12)*. When I was weary and worn down by hurt due to my loss, God provided me with true comfort. God welcomes us to rest in Him when we are tired and need peace.

In my mourning, my belief in Christ tremendously affected my journey of grief. My spiritual life has deepened and has been renewed as a result of my loss. I felt close to God and my prayer is that He gives you the power of His presence and peace. The mourning of losing a loved one does not signify that God is not with you. With the Word of God being your spiritual comfort and support, be reminded that *"He is with you always, to the end of the age" (Matthew 28:20)*.

God will provide the comfort that you need you're your heart is hurting so badly that you can barely breathe, move, or talk. He will carry you through the good and bad times. He will provide your every need and accomplish His great works on this journey. Ask God for comfort. At some point, the tears will subside, and the mornings will bring smiles. It is a process. Go through it.

God's words comforted my soul, *"weeping may endure for a night, but joy comes in the morning" (Psalm 30:5).* He will send others your way. He will give you the words to say. The support of others will work for you and fit your individual grief need. My hope is that you receive the strength you need in your hard times of grief and that God sends the great help of a support system who understands your needs.

5

Beyond the Tears

"Be merciful to me, Lord, for I am distress, my eyes grow weak with sorrow, my soul and body with grief."

-Psalm 31:9 (NIV)

~PRAYER to PRAY~

God, I thank You for being gracious to me. I need You as I embark on this unfamiliar journey of grief. Thank You for hearing my prayers. I thank You for wiping my tears. I am aware that I am not alone. Lift me out of any depression that is keeping me from a total healing and release Your oil of joy in my life. Your grace is sufficient for me. Thank You for Your grace and mercy. I need You in every second and minute of each day. In Jesus' name, Amen.

The tears would not stop falling during the day or at night. I did not want to think about my sister because she was gone. Thinking was not going to bring her back. Thinking of her brought too many sad feelings and it refreshed the hurt parts of grief. I missed her deeply, and could not help but to think of her. My eyes could not stop the tears. Many thoughts traveled my mind. How was I going to get through this without her? I thought this many times. She was my "to go to" person. There were more tears and sadness as the days went by.

I was in a depressive stage of my grief. I felt as if it would last forever. I was determined not to allow depression to defeat me. *On Grief and Grieving: Finding the Meaning of Grief through the Five Stages of Loss (2005),* Elisabeth Kubler-Ross and David Kessler stated that it is important to understand that this depression is not a sign of mental illness. "It is the appropriate response to great loss."

I was fully aware that sadness and tears were normal; still I did not want to be sad. I did not want to feel anything. I wanted it to all to go away. However, it did not work like that. I had to go through this stage of grief. It was not a pleasurable experience, but I made it through. Kubler-Ross and Kessler describe sadness in grief as one of the many necessary steps you have to endure to heal from grief.

It is important for you to know that you have the right to hurt and you have the right to heal. The significance of the loss you have experienced can determine the greatness of your emotions. My expression of my grief is how deeply I loved my sister. Everyone grieves differently and in his or her own time. There is no right or wrong way to grieve. Grievers need time to grieve as normal and natural as possible. The normal feelings of sadness that comes with grief has to take place. It is in the hardest parts of our grief where we need God the most. The physical symptoms are not a sign of weakness. These symptoms are an identification that you are moving through the stages of grief.

Tears are a part of your healing process. Tears are an expression of grief. Allow yourself time to cry. Do not deny yourself the ability to feel. This was a difficult process for me, but a much needed and important process. I could no longer suppress my feelings.

I knew that God was with me. I prayed to Him morning, day, and night. I cried out to Him, asking for His help to soothe the distress. He was indeed gracious to my needs of distress by providing me with comfort. The Lord is close to those who are suffering. I am certain that the grace of God strengthens me. I would have drowned in my grief without relying on God's Power.

Time has passed; I am in a new place after the loss of my sister. The sadness and tears come and go, but they are not as frequent as in the beginning. Writing this book has brought many tears; however, I am aware of the importance of allowing myself to feel and go through the process.

You can rest in the knowledge that God is near, and He gave us the Holy Spirit to help us. Make the conscious decision to allow Him to carry you and comfort you. He will wipe every tear away and give strength to your body. May He give you freedom from the pains of grief with the peace of His presence.

6

Peace He Gives

"Casting all your cares [all your anxieties, all your worries, and all your concerns, once and for all] on Him, for He cares about you [with deepest affection, and watches over you very carefully]." -1Peter 5:7 (AMP)

~PRAYER to PRAY~

Lord, I thank You for caring for me. I do not have the strength. I do not understand. I do not know how to move on after losing my loved one. I give You all my cares and my worries concerning my grief. I know You care for me. I thank You for the peace You give. As I continue to live in You, renew my spirit as I move forward. Keep my heart and mind focused on You. In Jesus' name, Amen.

How do I keep going after this tough loss? What do I do next? How do I live without one of the closest persons to me? Many questions boggled my mind. I did not want to keep going. I did not know what to do next. I was filled with numerous uncertainties. She was the only one who could care for me in the way she did. Worry began to consume my daily functioning and activities. There were times when I was so consumed with my grief that I could barely tend to the needs of my husband and three sons. I wasn't able to be there like I thought I should for anyone else in my family either. I did not know what to expect. The way I was feeling after losing my sister was unsettling and frightening. It was difficult knowing that my sister would never come home. I desperately desired to get through this and wanted practical ways to survive daily. I craved for peace. I knew I couldn't function without it.

Grief is difficult. As you go through the process of grief and healing many unexpected emotions and feelings will gradually creep in. Trying to balance the feelings of pain and loss while moving forward with everyday life is a challenge, yet it is attainable. Grief does not go away by denying it or avoiding it. We have to learn how to cope.

For many days and nights, I prayed for peace and that the Lord would keep my mind. Several times, I felt that I was about to lose my mind. I did not know how to go on through the confusion, the pain, and the anger. I was determined to search for the steps to continue to live life. I had hope. I did not stop praying. I began to be specific in my prayers. I was relentless in my call to serve God. I had to let God know that I could not make it without Him. I talked to Him in detail about my many feelings and fears, specifically asking Him for peace of mind.

Grief is not a disorder. It is not a disease or a sign of weakness. It is an emotional, physical, and spiritual necessity to healing. You have to grieve to heal. It is important for you to feel your grief. You will eventually find joy in life in the new ways you invent.

The peace that God gives kept my sanity. Faith plays a huge role in embracing grief moments. Although you feel like you are going crazy, you really are not going crazy. You are on the road to healing. Many others have had to travel this same road, and they survived grief. You too can go through grief to healing. I urge you to keep going. Do not give up. You will develop courage that you did not know you had. God will bless you with the peace you need to go through. *"Then you will experience God's peace, which exceeds anything we can understand. His peace will guard your hearts and minds as you live in Christ Jesus"* (Philippians 4:7, NLT).

The calmness that He provides is inexpressible. He will protect your heart and mind from the hard hit of the unbearable grief. Cry out to Him as much as you need to and for whatever you need to do. You will experience God's peace.

I was glad that my life was steered toward God. Prayer was my pathway to coping with grief. To be able to survive grief, I encourage you to turn to God and give your worries to Him. His Word provides comfort and guidance even on the lowest days. Even in your worries, He will show you that He cares. Receive Him. He will remind you of His presence in the little things in life. Look for something positive each day, even if some days you have to look a little harder.

I say to you, *"Now may the Lord of peace Himself give you His peace at all times and in every situation. The Lord be with all you all"* (2 Thessalonians 3:16, NLT).

7

Strength of My Heart

"My flesh and my heart may fail, but God is the rock and strength of my heart and my portion forever."

-Psalm 73:26 (AMP)

~PRAYER to PRAY~

Father God, thank You for being my portion and my strength. Your grace and power amazes me. Fill me up with more of You on this journey of grief. As my heart cries out to You, give me the strength to go on this unfamiliar journey. You are with me and I appreciate Your presence. I love how You grace me with your warm embrace of comfort and relief, even in my tears. Even in my hurt, You are still God. I recognize that Your strength is made perfect in my tears, my pain, and my hopeless and helpless times. Thank You Father. In Jesus' name, Amen.

Many times I wanted to give up on this newfound "moving forward" grief journey. It was new and unfamiliarly uncomfortable. I was experiencing waves of intense grief that felt like a rollercoaster ride that I did not enjoy at all. Oftentimes, you may feel helpless and powerless. I wondered, *"Was there anything I could have done to stop her from dying?"* I thought, *"Maybe if I was there, she would have been able to have the strength to hold on."* I felt like I failed her as a sibling. However, I knew it was all beyond my control. This was a reality I had to accept, that neither her life nor death were in my hands. Thankfully, these feelings were temporary and natural. At the time, I did not acknowledge these feelings. I tried to stay strong, but my grief process took the course. Eventually, I acknowledged and allowed unwanted, but necessary, feelings to take place. I have learned that this was a normal part of grieving.

The feelings of a broken heart came often for me. My heart and spirit cried. Our physical and emotional pains are the perfect situations for God to work His miraculous power and healing. God will provide you with the spiritual comfort your soul needs.

The Bible has many examples of grieving people who voiced their painful emotions. Lament is a passionate expression of grief or sorrow. It means reacting to a pain you can't control just as the state I found myself in.

Express to God in your deepest expression how you may feel alone, rejected, hopeless, tired, and/or afraid. Call on God to work on your behalf. Ask Him to rescue you and to restore your life. Allow Him into your deepest feelings, and let Him lead this way. This is a part of your healing. He will ease your sorrow. Let Him in.

Grief affects us in every aspect of our lives. Our lives are different and forever changed. As time goes on, grief softens and the intensity of the feelings come less often. However, it can come back to us at any time and the intensity will vary. Allow yourself time to think and to feel your way through the process. Experience it fully. Express it in your own unique way. God's strength is at its best when you need it the most.

Through all of the hurt, hopelessness, and tears, it is the power of the Holy Spirit that gives us the strength to keep going. The power of Jesus will sustain you when nothing else can. Grief is too big for you to handle on your own and has the capacity to drown you if you don't reach for your safety in God. The Lord says in Isaiah 43:2 (NIV), *"When you go through the deep waters, I will be with you. When you go through rivers of difficulty, you will not drown. When you walk through the fire of oppression, you will not be burned up, the flames will not consume you."*

Allow God to be your strength and portion as you go through the process. His grace is more than enough for you in your weakest moments. Press through the pain, the hurt, and tears. Take Him at His Word. Let the Holy Spirit fill your emptiness with His Spirit of love and power.

8

Move Forth in the Valley

"The Lord is my Shepard, I lack nothing. He makes me to lie down in green pastures, He leads me beside quiet waters, and He refreshes my soul. He guides me along the right paths for His name's sake. Even though I walk through the darkest valley, I will fear no evil, for you are with me: your rod and your staff, they comfort me." - Psalm 23:1-4 (NIV)

~PRAYER to PRAY~

Father, I thank You for the grace You give. You are the strength of my life. I appreciate Your amazing grace and Your healing power. Thank You for Your comfort. Thank You for being with me in the valley as I go through and move forth after losing my loved one. I want to heal and move forward to a renewed life after loss. I know that I am not alone because You are with me in this process and in everything I encounter. In Jesus' name, Amen.

As I look back on the beginning of my grief journey, I reflect on the lowest points of my grief. Without a shadow of doubt, I know God hands of protection are keeping me. In the beginning, I could not see my way through my grief. However, I was determined to move forward no matter how badly I hurt. It was in my valley that I searched for more from God and for Him to hold me up both physically and spiritually. Even in the valley, I asked God to show me how to get through this unfamiliar path. So many unanswered questions. I had comfort in knowing that God was with me on this new walk. I embraced each moment with Him and gained revelation of His wonderful glory.

Grief is unpredictable. Grief is overwhelming. Grief is a part of life and loss. There are many strategies to coping with grief, and everyone has their own way to overcome. There are healthy and unhealthy ways of coping. While in darkest moments of your grief, it can be easy to use negative coping skills, which can be described as an emotional pain reliever that numbs the pain temporarily, eventually the pain appears. You can survive grief with a permanent pain relief, which is Jesus Christ's power of healing and wholeness. Allow the light of God to shine in the darkest parts of this unfamiliar journey.

You may find yourself in places of your grief where you do not want to be. This does not mean that you are in the wrong place. You are actually in the right place for God's rod and staff to comfort you. Your way to finding life after loss is directed toward God. You do not have to walk on this path alone. Expand your boundaries and let God step in to heal your brokenness due to grief. Continue to move forth in the valley of your grief. Allow God to protect you. Do not be afraid because He is with you.

Dealing with the loss of my sister has not been comfortable. The suffering cut to the core of my heart, and I had my share of emotions and pain. I thought the dark days would never end. However, my relationship with God kept me leveled. I did not want to suffer anymore from the loss of my dear sister. I wanted God to be glorified in my suffering. By God's generous grace, I became stronger. I was not sure in the beginning; however, I strived to become knowledgeable about God's healing power as my grieving forward journey unfolded.

Anyone who has been faced with grief will react in their own way. The intensity of grief symptoms may come and go. Grieving is a way of showing how we feel and allowing ourselves time to fully experience our loss. Prolonged suffering prevents our grief process from moving forward into acceptance. The suffering will not last forever. It is important to heal from loss and to take the process seriously.

Although the healing process is hard, it is good! It is where God works. Be willing to be open and honest to God and yourself. Look for God in the midst of your suffering. We may not understand, but there is significant purpose, even in hurt. There is purpose in your pain, which God alone knows and will definitely lead you. Allow God to bring you from the darkness into the light of healing. Look for Him after your loss. That is where you will find Him, and He will build you up again. He will make you strong and steady. May God's grace be with you. *"And the God of all grace, who called you to His eternal glory in Christ, after you have suffered a little while, will himself restore you and make you strong, firm, and steadfast"* (1 Peter 5:10, NIV).

9

Take It to God in Prayer

"Don't worry about anything; instead, pray about everything. Tell God what you need and thank Him for all He has done." -Philippians 4:6 (NLT)

~PRAYER to PRAY~

Lord, I want to thank You for releasing me from the fear of what is to come after my loss. Even on this process, I trust You more than ever before. I thank You for being my strength. I do not understand why, but I know that You have a plan for me. At this time, I am hurting and I need Your Comfort. It feels like these hurtful feelings will never go away. I cannot imagine going through this without You holding me up. This is hard to face or even to look for tomorrow. I'm not sure of how I will get through this day without (name loved one) in my life. I need You to help me continue to move forward in my life. In Jesus name, Amen.

Losing someone you love can challenge your faith. I had moments where I could not pray. There would be times where only prayer would give me the comfort that I needed. There is something about calling upon the Lord and telling Him how you are feeling and what you need. I went to God in prayer when I was angry, confused, sad, and needed guidance on how to move forward in the most difficult times of my grief. He answered my cries and led me through.

Losing a sibling has shown me how much I need to pray. Praying day to day was not enough. Talking to God was needed many times throughout the day. This passage in the Bible gave me hope, *"I prayed to the Lord, and He answered me. He freed me from all my fears" (Psalms 34:4, NLT).* Remain consistent in praying to God. It is the foundation needed to go through your grief journey. I could not pray just for myself, also for others that have experience the loss of a loved one just as well. I often pray that God's comfort will be extended to my family and others who have experienced the death of a loved one. Being up close and personal with grief, I understand the pain that it brings into a person's life.

The Bible tells us about Job and how he lost all his possessions and his family. The Bible describes how Job *"tore his robe in grief" (Job 1:20, NLT).* Job did not hide his overwhelming grief. Yet, He did not lose his faith in God. He was human and his grief showed that he loved his family dearly. It is not inappropriate to express our emotions as Job did. Like many, Job was faced with the choice of having faith in God or to give up. His decision was to trust God. We must also trust God when we do not understand the difficulties we face.

When you experience loss, don't be afraid to express your deepest hurt to God and yourself. Allow yourself to grieve. You may not understand the pain you experience, allow it to lead you to a deeper relationship with God.

Prayer can help us move past the deep sense of anger and sadness into acceptance and living life. Prayer helps us to grow effectively with God. Ask God to be by your side through these times. Do not be afraid to be genuine with God about how you are feeling. He is waiting to hear from you.

Grab a pen and notebook and write to God about how you are feeling. Kneel before the Lord, or however you feel comfortable talking to God; and take it all to Him in prayer. Don't be afraid to be vulnerable in the presence of God by sharing how you truly feel about your loss. Tell your Heavenly Father what you need from Him.

Grief is one of the toughest battles I have had to face in life. I often thought that a bad day would never compare to my grief journey, not even a nightmare. A nightmare leaves you in fear, but eventually you wake up. Experiencing the death of a loved one is not something you can wake up from one day and grasp that it was only a dream. In the beginning stages of my grief journey, there were many fears and tears. I tried to ignore many feelings. I tried to push them aside and tried to hide it all away, but I could not. Feelings of grief kept coming. I continued to ask God for strength and wisdom on how to handle it all.

After the initial response to loss, fear can come forth as a normal reaction. Fear comes in many ways. You may be afraid to be alone, to meet new people, to talk about your loss loved one, or even afraid of death or dying. New fears will come to mind. It is common to feel uncertain of what the future holds and to be afraid of what your life would be like after your loss. Fear is just a reaction. Do not let it be a part of who you are.

Identify your fears and talk openly about them. Use a journal to write about your thoughts and feelings. Replace negative thoughts with scriptures that relates to what you're fading. Work through these grief concerns with a trusted person in your spiritual support system.

Take your concerns to God. Fear is an issue that many people deal with, and God is aware. Do not worry; God is never deaf to your prayers. He sees. He hears. He will definitely deliver you. Trust that He will answer you. Utilize your faith and trust that God will give you victory over the control of fear. He will provide you with peace. Allow Him to free you from your fears.

10

Gratitude in Grief

"I will praise the Lord at all times. I will constantly speak His praises." -Psalms 34:1(NLT)

~PRAYER to PRAY~

Lord, I want to thank You for the good days and the not so good days. Thank You for not letting me drown in my grief. Thank You for showing me the sunshine in the storm of my sadness. I am indeed grateful for all things. Lord, thank You for planting in me the fight to go on. Please continue to be with me as I learn new ways of living without my loved one. Guide my steps as I take new paths on this journey. In Jesus' name, Amen.

I have many reasons to be thankful to God. Prior to my sister's transition from earth to heaven, I realized during the duration of her illness, I grieved. Grieving her illness was nothing compared to losing her. The stages of grief were prevalent, and I experienced intense feelings then. I understand that her sickness caused her physical body to be weary. As I watched God care for her during the roughest days of her sickness, I was thankful for Him caring for her in the way that He did.

I am reminded of a visit that our family received as we made preparation for her funeral. My sister's Bishop and Pastor of her church home visited our home and spoke many words that encouraged us through one of the hardest tasks ever. Their encouraging words helped me to gain a spiritual understanding of my sister's death. Understanding that her transition from earth to heaven can be viewed as her being gone on a "trip." She left on her journey to Heaven before we did. We will meet her there one day. She got to Heaven before us. When we get to Heaven, we will be able to see her again. Heaven is a place that I am striving to get to one day.

I have peace knowing that she transitioned to Heaven, even though her presence is no longer with us. I found much gratitude in knowing that even in the six years after being diagnosed with a heart problem, she was able to live a fulfilling life. I could not be selfish about my desires and not consider that God's plan for her life and mine were not the same. I could not bargain with Him or be angry with Him for what He allowed to happen. I had to trust Him fully.

Bless the Lord while going through your grief process. Giving God praises for the things that He has already done helps to lighten the difficult moments. Find joy in the faithful God that you serve. Think on some of the positive things that He has done in this day and receive His strength to get through this journey.

I encourage you to find out what works best for you to keep pressing forward. What kept me moving forward is that I wanted to honor God by trusting Him. Also, I wanted to honor the life that my sister lived. She lived a life full of perseverance with much passion and love for others, despite her weaknesses. I watched how she cared for her only daughter, Sa'Nya and shared love and compassion to many others. That was enough motivation for me to keep going on.

We have to understand that grief does not just end, and we do not "get over" losing a loved one. We have to believe that God is a Healer. By faith, we can be whole after loss. The death of a loved one is something we learn to live with over time.

Embrace your grief process. Although, the reactions and feelings of grief may revisit us at any time, we are aware of the knowledge and spiritual wisdom of how to survive and continue to press whenever we are reminded of our loved one.

While grief brings many uncertainties, there is a renewed life and revelation awaiting. You will develop a renewed sense of significance and purpose. You have to press your way through the hard parts of your grief. Have faith in God that you can develop the resilience you need to be restored. God understands your fight. He will help you find the inner strength to endure during this hardship. *Philippians 3:14 says, "I press on to reach the end of the race and receive the heavenly prize for which God, through Christ Jesus, is calling us" (NLT).*

11

Renewed Life

"But those who wait for the Lord [who expect, look for, and hope in Him] will gain new strength and renew their power; They will lift up their wings [and rise up close to God] like eagles [rising toward the sun]; They will run and not become weary, They will walk and not grow tired.

-Isaiah 40:31(AMP)

~PRAYER to PRAY~

Lord, I want to thank You for being my backbone on this tedious journey. Help me to take You at Your word and accept the renewed strength of life you have offered me. Give me the strength daily. Comfort me always. I trust that You are ordering my steps, one step and one moment at a time. I thank You for everything I have endured to move me closer to my healing. In Jesus' name, Amen.

I truly believe that my sister has found her place of belonging. After a long physical battle of sickness, Shanika

Thames had a relationship with our Savior. I have great comfort knowing that she belonged to God, who is more powerful than anything. She is resting peacefully in His bosom. My trust in Him required me to wait patiently on Him, even in my most difficult times on this journey. He allowed me to go through the process of grief without Him missing a step from being by my side, moment by moment. I am able to go forth in life without the weariness and burden of anger, bitterness, and depression because of the loss of my loved one.

Do not get tired of giving Him the hurt days, sad days, or any other concerns you may have. Continue to give it all to Him as it comes to you. My desire is to move forward and to continue to honor God and the life my sister lived. She left with us many valuable lessons to remember and follow. She was a genuine person who always found time to give unselfishly to others. Even during the six years of living with postpartum cardio myopathy, she exemplified many Godly characteristics. In the years of her sickness, it was a physical, mental, and spiritual strain on her. I watched what she went through. The mental and physical effects of her sickness took a toll on her. I felt helpless. Yet, many times God restored her mind and body. I witnessed how she was strong in the Lord. She endured several illnesses caused by her heart condition and had to take many medications that resulted in more illnesses from time to time.

Many people were unaware of her illness. That is how she lived her life. This was not because she was ashamed of her physical state, but because she did not want to be identified as her illness. She was a firm believer of Christ. She wanted others to see past her sickness and to witness her God-given purpose and plan for her life. I did not understand this in the beginning, but this revelation unfolded during the completion of writing this book. Although our loved one is no longer with us, their memories will live on forever. Allow yourself the opportunity of reflection and remembrance.

My grief journey required a relationship with God. I am not sure of how I could make it this far without my knowledge of Him and His promises and assurance to take care of all my concerns and me. Nurture your physical, emotional, and spiritual needs by maintaining the needs of each. This includes, but not is limited to, resting, nutrition, exercise, expressing thoughts and feelings, and including God in the process.

As you walk into acceptance on this journey, continue to persevere. Though it may be a rocky road, you can still move along this road with God. You can still stand up and make steps to heal. Continue to hold on to your faith in God. If I can get through, I know that you can too.

I want to encourage you to cling to God's Word as if it is the breath you need for your body. Search for Him on this journey. You will find Him. *"The Lord is near to all who call on Him" (Psalm 145:18, NLT).* Rest in the comfort of knowing that He will never leave you or forsake you. Take your healing one step at a time and one day at a time. You will move forward and rediscover meaning in your life.

May God give you everything you need on this journey of grief forward to healing. I pray that you receive every ounce of comfort, joy, strength, and peace in each grieving forward moment.

Notes

Elisabeth Kubler-Ross and David Kessler, On Grief and Grieving: Finding the Meaning of Grief through the Five Stages of Loss (New York, NY: Scribner, 2005).

About the Author

Shawanda Payne has a gift to encourage others. The Delta native delights herself in the Lord by studying the Word of God and intercession. She gracefully shares her personal experience with loss and grief to give others hope that surviving is attainable with the help of God's power and personal efforts.

Shawanda holds a Bachelor's degree in Social Work and more than eight years of experience of working in the mental health profession with a concentration in working with developmentally disabled individuals and those with mild to severe mental illnesses. Currently, she serves as a Program Director at an adult day services in her community. Grieving Forward: Embracing each Moment with God is Payne's debut into the publishing world.

When not working or volunteering, this girl-next-door can be found in one of her favorite places, spending time with her husband, Marcus and their three sons Jeremiah, Marcus Jr. and Sean --cup of coffee in hand. She strives to lift others up and share the love of Jesus and her love for Him in her daily walk. She joyfully serves as an intercessor and as a teacher with the youth ministry at The Carpenter's Church.